SPOTLIGHT ON NATIONS

# MEXICO

NELL MUSOLF

CREATIVE EDUCATION · CREATIVE PAPERBACKS

Published by Creative Education and Creative Paperbacks
P.O. Box 227, Mankato, Minnesota 56002
Creative Education and Creative Paperbacks are imprints
of The Creative Company
www.thecreativecompany.us

Design and production by Tom Morgan
Art direction by Blue Design, Inc.
Edited by Ana Brauer

Photographs by Dreamstime/Timothy Stirling, 14; Pexels/Mikhail Nilov, cover, 1; Unsplash/Abhi Verma, 28, Angels for Humanity, 29, Cody McLain, 2–3, Danie Franco, 23, Emmanuel Acua, 26, Eugenio B, 15, Evan Wise, 18, Jeremy Lwanga, 27, Jimmy Woo, 24, Kiernan James, 4–5, Kyle Petzer, 30, Prachi sharma, 21, Yucel Moran, 9; Wikimedia Commons/Alex Covarrubias, 8, 10, 14, 16, 20, 22, Guillermo Kahlo, 21, Henry R. Robinson, 17, José Luiz Bernardes Ribeiro / CC BY-SA 4.0, 16, NASA, 12, Presidencia de Guatemala, 6, public domain, 11, Walter Rodriguez, 10



Library of Congress Cataloging-in-Publication Data
Names: Musolf, Nell author
Title: Mexico / by Nell Musolf.
Description: Mankato, Minnesota : Creative Education and Creative Paperbacks, [2026] | Series: Spotlight on nations | Includes bibliographical references and index. | Audience: Ages 10–13 | Audience: Grades 4–6 | Summary: "Explore Mexico's history, government, economy, cultural heritage, family dynamics, and modern challenges, plus its diverse landscapes and efforts toward economic stability. Written for middle-grade readers, this book includes timelines, sidebars, glossary, resources, and index"— Provided by publisher.
Identifiers: LCCN 2025016993 (print) | LCCN 2025016994 (ebook) | ISBN 9798895810736 library binding | ISBN 9798896800262 paperback | ISBN 9798895811993 ebook
Subjects: LCSH: Mexico—Juvenile literature | Mexico—Civilization | Mexico—History | Mexico—Description and travel
Classification: LCC F1208.5 .M87 2026 (print) | LCC F1208.5 (ebook) | DDC 972—dc23/eng/20250610
LC record available at https://lccn.loc.gov/2025016993
LC ebook record available at https://lccn.loc.gov/2025016994

Printed in the United States

# CONTENTS

INTRODUCTION

# MEXICO'S COASTS

Mexico is a large country in North America. It is the third-largest country in Latin America, after Brazil and Argentina. Mexico shares a northern border with the United States and a southern border with Belize and Guatemala. The Gulf of Mexico is on the east side of Mexico and the Pacific Ocean is on its west. Approximately 130 million people live in Mexico. About 80 percent of the population lives in big cities located in the middle of the country. The people living in rural areas often maintain traditional lifestyles similar to those of their **ancestors** hundreds of years ago. Mexico is a beautiful country, but it has problems, including the gap between the very rich and the very poor. The government struggles to make life more **equitable** for all the people who live in Mexico. But despite its problems, Mexicans are proud of their history and of their homeland.

CLOSE-UP

## Going Down?

Mexico City is built on land that was once a lake. Because the ground underneath the city is soft and made of clay, parts of it are sinking at a rate of almost 20 inches (50.8 centimeters) a year.

CHAPTER ONE

# HISTORY OF MEXICO

Mexico's history goes back thousands of years. Several Native American cultures lived in Mexico. Two of the largest cultures were the Mayans and the Aztecs.

The Mayans built temples and pyramids out of stone. They grew crops on land that was once a rainforest. The Mayans also had their own writing system. It was called **hieroglyphics**. Mayans studied the planets and stars. They created an extremely accurate calendar.

The Aztec Empire was the last large civilization before the Spanish arrived in the 1500s. The Aztecs were farmers, fishers, and hunters. They created a strong military that helped them become powerful rulers.

Spanish explorer Hernán Cortés arrived in Mexico in 1519. The Aztec people believed Cortés was a god named Quetzalcoatl. Quetzalcoatl was a vegetation god who ruled earth and water. The Aztecs didn't fight Cortés

MILESTONES IN MEXICO'S HISTORY

**1500 BC**

- Olmecs live in villages in what is now southern Mexico

**250–900**

- Maya cities are established in south Mexico

since they thought he was the god brought back to life. In 1521, Cortés conquered Tenochtitlan, the Aztec capital, and the Aztec rule ended. What had been the Aztec Empire became part of Spain. Cortés named the country New Spain.

Under Spanish rule, many things changed. The Spaniards took control of the native tribes and ruled for 300 years. The Spaniards brought many diseases with them, including smallpox. Between 7 and 18 million native people became sick and died from these diseases. As the years passed, the desire to be independent of Spanish rule grew stronger among the indigenous people. Slowly, they began to fight the Spanish to get their land back.

CLOSE-UP

## Chocolate

The Olmec civilization is believed to be one of the first to use cacao, the plant from which chocolate is made. Chocolate was used during religious rituals and as medicine. A few centuries later, the Mayans called chocolate the drink of the gods.

The Mexican War of Independence began in 1810. An army of peasants—composed of indigenous people and **mestizos**—began a march to Mexico

## Nahuatl

**There are 68 different languages and 364 dialects in Mexico. One language that is still spoken stretches back to the Aztec people. It is called Nahuatl. Nahuatl was first spoken in central Mexico in the seventh century B.C. Nahuatl became the most dominant language in central Mexico. It also adopted many Spanish words over time. Some Nahuatl words became part of the English language. Chili, chocolate, coyote, avocado, and guacamole are words that were originally Nahuatl. In 2025, approximately 1.5 million people, mainly in Central Mexico, still spoke Nahuatl.**

City. On August 16, 1821, Mexico declared its independence from Spain.

In 1846, war broke out between Mexico and the United States. It was over a border dispute between the two countries. The conflict was called the Mexican-American War. The war lasted two years. When it was over, the United States gained large parts of Mexico, including the present states of Nevada, Utah, Arizona, Colorado, California, New Mexico, and Wyoming.

The 20th century brought a lot of change. Mexico's economy improved because it had a more stable government. From the 1940s to the 1970s, the people of Mexico had more money to spend, and their lifestyles were better than they had ever been before. However, a new problem came up: illegal drugs. Drugs were sold throughout Mexico and to other countries. Drug dealers and their **cartels** caused violence in the cities. The drug problem became so bad that the government had to create programs to fight back against the dealers.

**600**

- Mayan and Teotihuacán cultures begin to lose power

**900**

- Toltec civilization gains power

CLOSE-UP

## Am I Blue?

Lakes are always blue, right? Nope! Pink lakes called Las Coloradas are at the end of the Yucatán Peninsula and the water looks pink. Red algae and brine shrimp live in the lakes and cause the water to look pink.

HISTORICAL HIGHLIGHT

## Immigration

The term "immigration" is used when a person moves from one country to another permanently. Immigration between the United States and Mexico has been a hot topic for almost 200 years. When people hear the word immigration, most of them think of Mexican people immigrating to the United States. But in 1830, Mexico banned immigration to Texas, which was then a part of Mexico. The government wanted to stop English-speaking settlers from moving permanently to their country.

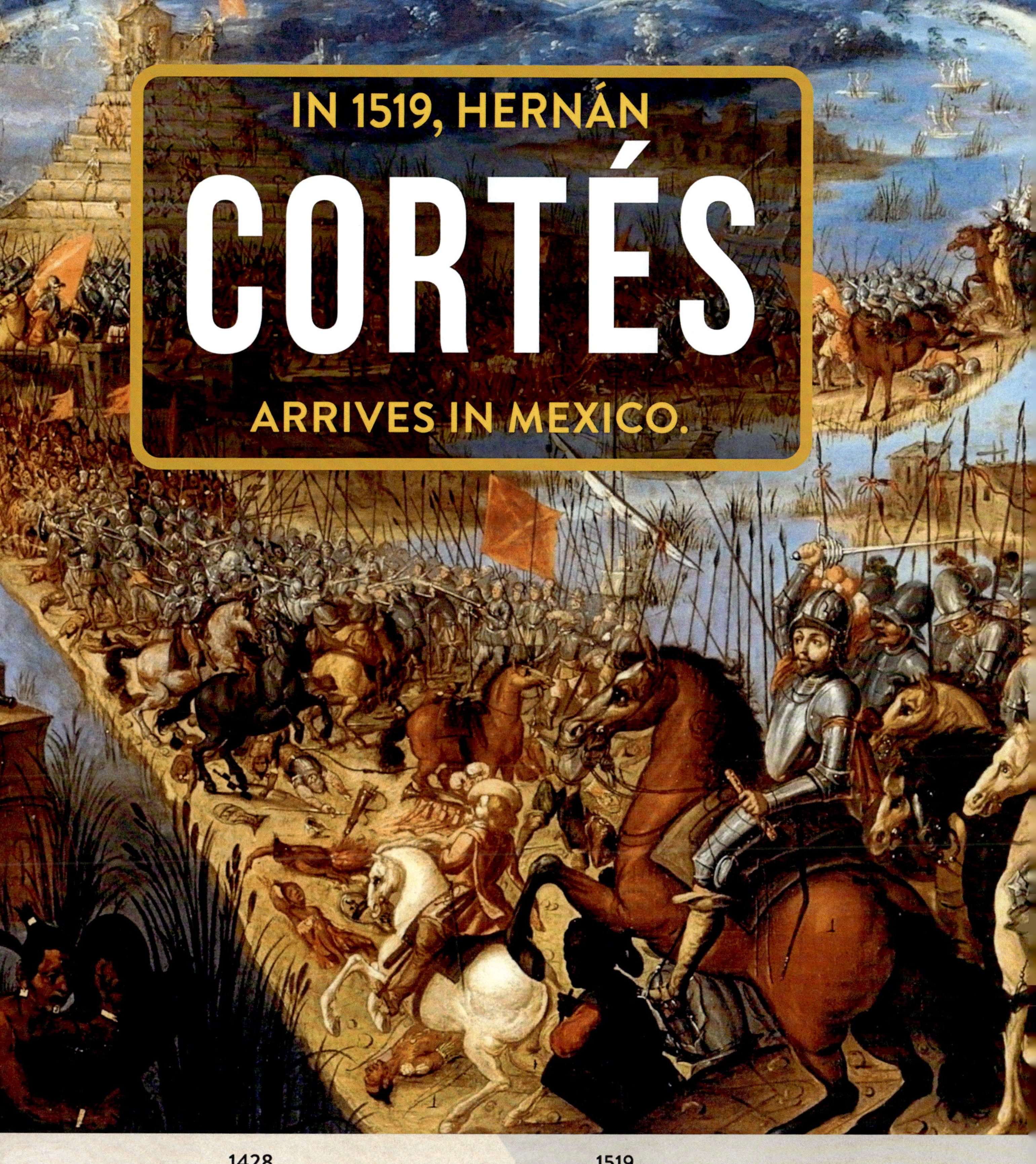

# IN 1519, HERNÁN CORTÉS ARRIVES IN MEXICO.

**1428**

- Aztecs gain control of central Mexico

**1519**

- Hernán Cortés arrives in Mexico from Cuba

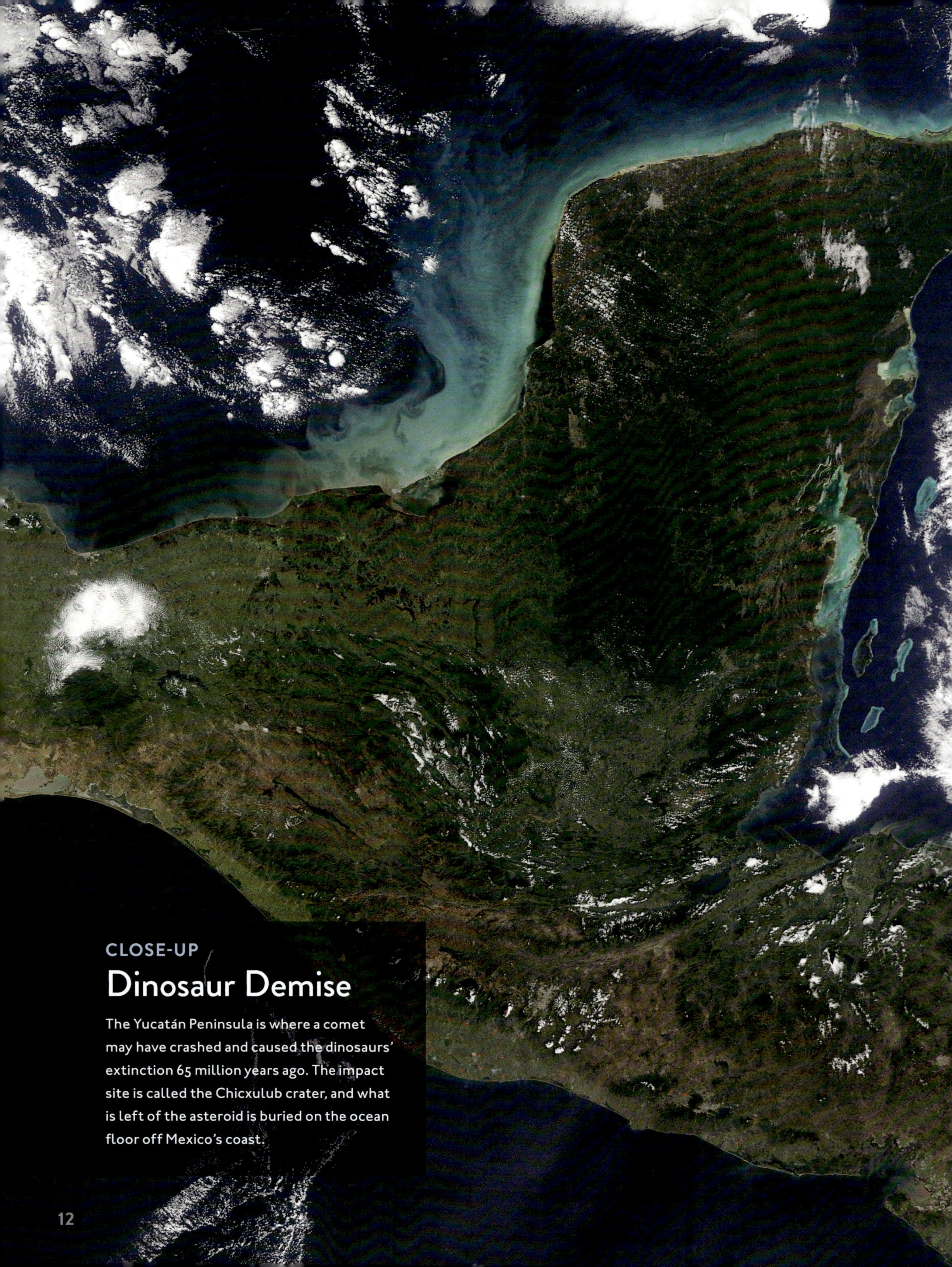

CLOSE-UP

## Dinosaur Demise

The Yucatán Peninsula is where a comet may have crashed and caused the dinosaurs' extinction 65 million years ago. The impact site is called the Chicxulub crater, and what is left of the asteroid is buried on the ocean floor off Mexico's coast.

CHAPTER TWO

# GOVERNMENT AND ECONOMY

Mexico's official name is the United Mexican States. Mexico is a federal republic. Its 1917 constitution says that power in Mexico is divided among three branches. The branches are the Presidency, the Congress, and the Courts.

The president is elected by the people. Whoever receives the most votes in the national election wins. Presidents serve a single six-year term. They cannot be re-elected. Each president appoints his or her **cabinet**. The cabinet helps the president run the country.

Congress is divided into a Chamber of Deputies and a Senate. There are 300 deputies who are elected every three years. There are 128 senators who are elected every six years. Senators and deputies make new laws and update old laws.

Mexico has 31 states and one federal district. There are three government levels: central, state, and local. Every state elects its governor and congress. Each city has an elected mayor.

**1521**

- Cortés defeats the Aztec capital and begins to build Mexico City on its ruins

**1521–1820**

- Mexico becomes part of the Viceroyalty of New Spain

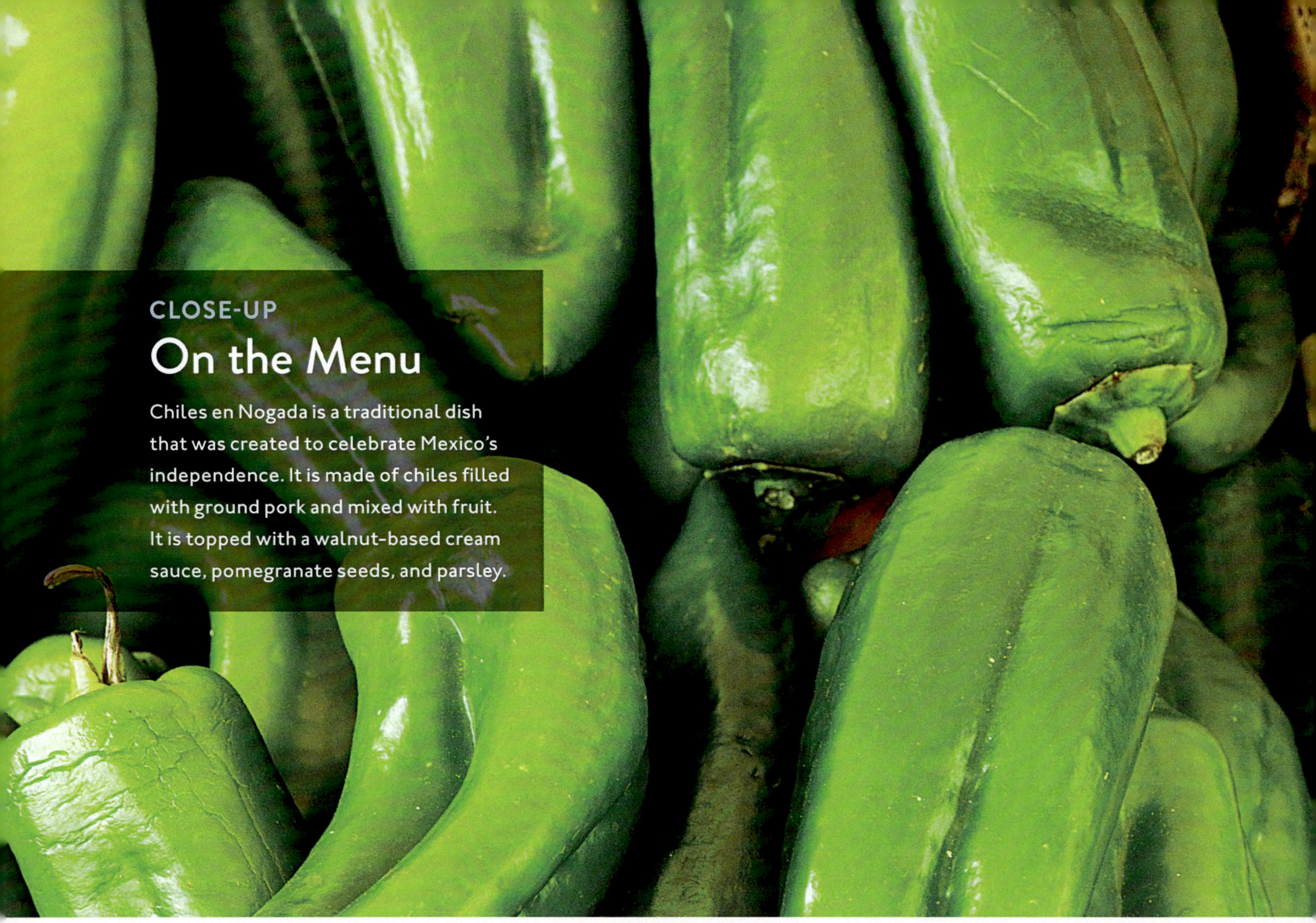

CLOSE-UP

## On the Menu

Chiles en Nogada is a traditional dish that was created to celebrate Mexico's independence. It is made of chiles filled with ground pork and mixed with fruit. It is topped with a walnut-based cream sauce, pomegranate seeds, and parsley.

## Rare Crops

Mexico grows two crops that are rarely found in any other part of the world. One is called henequén. It is grown in Yucatán and produces a strong fiber. Henequén goes back to the Mayans. It was made into rope for ships, fibers used in furniture, and cloth sacks. It was exported to North America but when synthetic fibers were invented, demand for henequén went down. The second crop unique to Mexico is maguey. It is used in alcoholic beverages.

There are currently four dominant political parties in Mexico. The Institutional Revolutionary Party (PRI) was formed in 1920 to try and stop violence among political groups. The National Action Party (PAN) began in 1939 as the opposition party to the PRI. The Party of the Democratic Revolution (PRD) started in 1986 as a democratic reform party promoting openness. The largest political party is the Morena party. It was founded in 2014 with an anti-corruption agenda. Mexico's current president, Claudia Sheinbaum, is a member of the Morena party.

Mexico's economy is the second-largest in Latin America after Brazil's. Mexico has a large population and many natural resources. It has an open trade policy and it manufactures goods for countries around the world.

Mexico's economy has struggled since 1980. Between 1980 and 2022, it grew two percent every year, and growth continues to be slow. However, the poverty rate dropped from more than 40 percent in 2020 to 36 percent in 2022. Despite that, millions of people remain poor.

Tourism is one Mexico's main industries. People travel from around the world to visit Mexico's beaches, archaeological sites, and cities. With so many tourists, the service industry is one of the country's main employers. Service industry jobs include hotel workers, restaurant employees, and tour guides.

Mexico produces corn, coffee, sugar cane, beans, tomatoes, and avocados. Bananas, pineapples, mangoes, and other tropical produce grow in Mexico. Oil, copper, gold, silver, and zinc are produced in Mexico. During the 1980s, oil was the strongest industry. Now manufactured goods are strongest and make up 80 percent of exports.

**1821**

- War of Independence ends. For a short while, Mexico is known as the Mexican Empire

**1824**

- Mexico becomes a federal republic

CLOSE-UP

## Temple Ruins

The Aztecs built temples to their gods, where priests made human sacrifices. One of the most famous temples is Templo Mayor in Mexico City. Visitors can see the ruins of this ancient temple today.

## Copper Canyon

Mexico's many mountains are home to several canyons, including Copper Canyon in Chihuahua, the largest state in Mexico. Copper Canyon is made up of six separate canyons, all of which are part of the Copper Canyon National Park. People travel there to ride on the scenic Copper Canyon train and take in the breathtaking views of the canyons. Copper Canyon covers 25,000 square miles (64,749 sq km). It is considerably larger than the Grand Canyon in the United States, which is 1,904 square miles (4,931 sq km) in size.

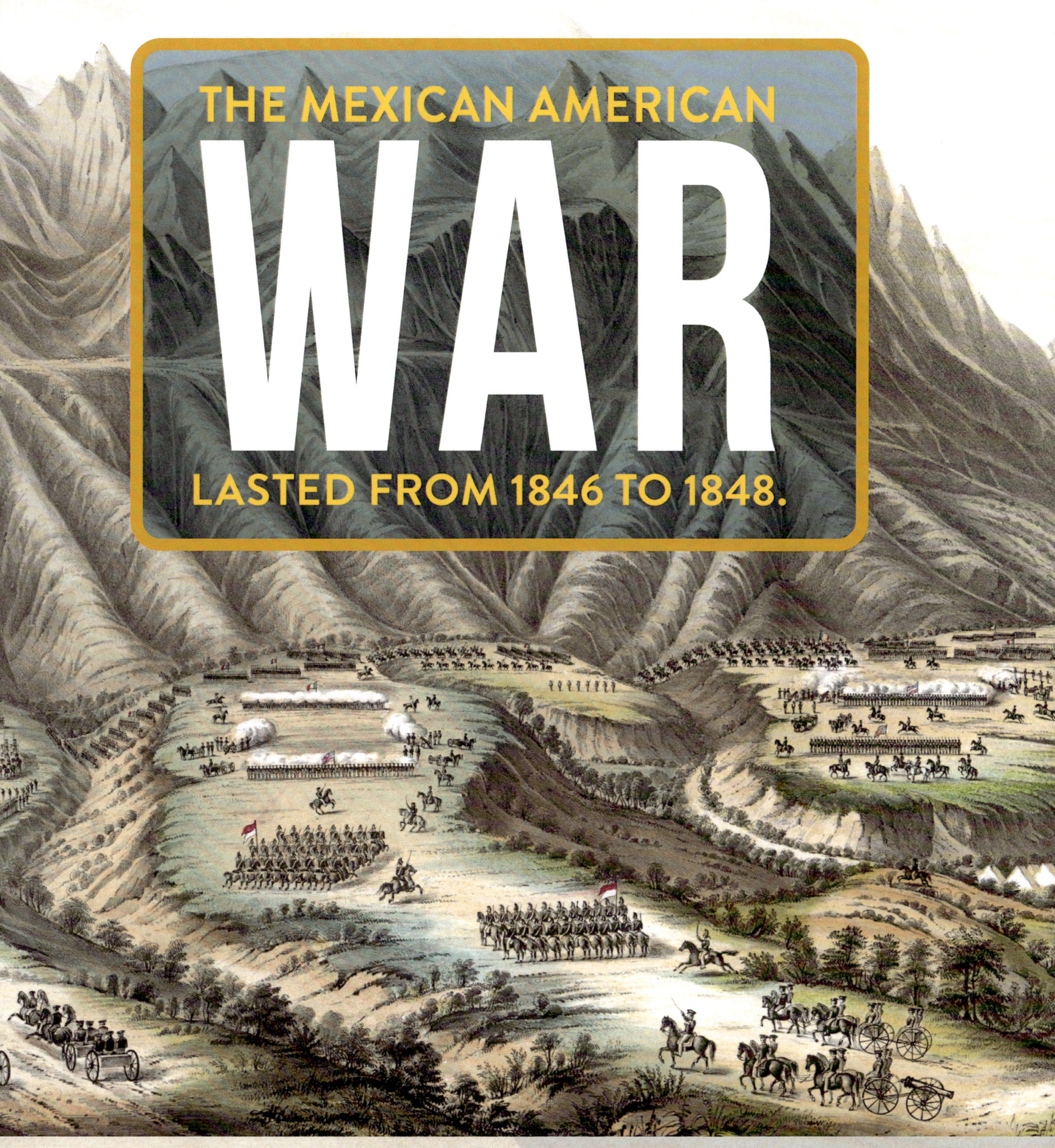


**1848**

- Mexican-American War ends, and Mexico is forced to sell much of its land to the U.S.

**1876–1911**

- Porfirio Díaz begins dictatorship of Mexico

## CLOSE-UP
# How Do You Say?

Mexico has 68 recognized languages. Most of those languages are indigenous. Four languages are known as language isolates. These are languages that aren't related to any other language.

CHAPTER THREE

# MEXICO'S PEOPLE AND CULTURE

Mexico is made up of different ethnic groups. The largest group is mestizos. Mestizos make up more than half of Mexico's population. Indigenous American Indians make up less than a tenth of the population.

Ethnicity is important to the people of Mexico. October 12 is the Día de la Raza, or "Race Day." People celebrate their heritage on Día de la Raza with parties, feasts, and bullfights.

Mexican families tend to be tightly knit. Most people count on their families for love and support and for a feeling of security. Children grow up surrounded by relatives who watch over them. Many Mexican families have relatives living with them beyond the **nuclear family**.

Grandparents might live with the family or live close by. Even after

**1920**

- Mexican Revolution ends Díaz's dictatorship and begins constitutional government
- The Institutional Revolutionary Party (PRI) is formed and dominates government for 71 years

children have grown up and married, their families still play a big part of their lives. Mexican families often spend time together, especially to celebrate holidays, birthdays, or other important events.

Students must attend primary school from ages 6 to 12. Middle school is divided into two stages. Grades seven through nine are called lower-secondary. Grades 10 through 12 are upper-secondary. Students choose either an academic track or a technical track. Students who choose the academic track often go on to college. The technical track focuses on **vocational** training.

Recent figures estimate about 36 percent of the population live below the poverty line. Many teenagers have part-time jobs to help their families and to earn money for themselves. The minimum age to work is 15. However, it is believed millions of children younger than age 15 work, some as young

## Quinceañera

**Turning 15 is an important milestone for girls in Mexico, celebrated with a quinceañera. "Quince" means fifteen in Spanish. The celebration marks the transition from childhood to womanhood. It usually begins with a Mass at church, followed by a party where family and friends have dinner, dance, and give gifts to the birthday girl. Girls celebrating their quinceañera wear elaborate gowns of satin and lace and are the queen of the day. They often share a special dance with their father or another close relative.**

CLOSE-UP

## Famous Frida

Frida Kahlo (1907–54) was a famous Mexican painter known for her colorful self-portraits. She wore bright clothes and flowers in her hair. Kahlo showed the world how important it is to be yourself and express your feelings through art.

**1968**

- Olympic Games held in Mexico City are interrupted by student demonstrations. Hundreds are killed or wounded

**1976**

- Oil is discovered off the coast of Mexico

as age seven. Children living in rural areas usually begin working earlier than children living in cities. Social programs are trying to help families by giving them money to keep their children in school.

Children often remain at home until they get married or find a job that requires them to move. Grown children help with household chores and contribute to the family's budget. Living at home is a normal way of life and usually only children from wealthy families leave home to go to college.

While many families struggle with poverty, their closeness and willingness to help each other in hard times make family ties stronger.

CLOSE-UP

## Taxi!

There are more taxicabs in Mexico than anywhere else in the world. Mexico has 60,000 registered taxis. Most are in Mexico City. Riding in a taxi in Mexico is cheaper than almost anywhere else in the world.

## Abuela

While all family members are important, grandmothers in Mexico— "abuelas"—hold a very special role. Abuelas are known as the keepers of family history. They work hard to make sure a family's heritage is passed down from one generation to the next. They remind their families how important their culture is, and how important it is to remember their culture. Abuelas are sometimes called the thread that connects generations. They have an important job that they take very seriously.

# LA FAMILIA ES LO MÁS IMPORTANTE

## FAMILY IS THE MOST IMPORTANT THING.

**2018**

- Mexico reaches a new trade deal with the U.S. and Canada

**2024**

- Claudia Sheinbaum Pardo is elected as Mexico's first woman president

CLOSE-UP

## Soft Drinks

Who doesn't like Coca-Cola? Many Mexican citizens love the popular soft drink. It is estimated 42 gallons (160 liters) are consumed annually per person. In some towns, soft drinks like Coca-Cola are more available than clean drinking water.

CHAPTER FOUR

# MEXICO TODAY

Mexico is a country of contrasts: wet rainforests and arid deserts, towering mountains and beaches, sparsely populated rural areas and densely populated cities, and both very wealthy people and those who are barely getting by. Mexico's future depends on its people working together.

Mexico faces many challenges due to its size and population. Some of the biggest challenges are human rights issues, like gender-based violence and attacks on journalists and human rights defenders. Pollution is another big problem. In the 1980s and 1990s, air pollution in Mexico City became so bad that it caused birds to fall out of the sky. Since then, the government has introduced an action plan that reduced air pollution by half. While pollution has lessened, fighting it is an ongoing challenge.

Crime is another problem. The government has been fighting drug cartels for more than 20 years. However, thousands of Mexican citizens die each year from homicide related to the cartels. Since 2006, almost half a million people have been killed in drug cartel battles. Mexico has partnered with the United States to fight the cartels, but success has been limited.

Mexico is one of the top tourist destinations in the world. In 2024,

45 million tourists traveled to Mexico. Having people visit brings millions of dollars into the country.

In addition to tourism, Mexico has become a hub for technology. In fact, Mexico's tech industry employs more than one million people. Experts expect technology to increase by as much as 12 percent by 2028. Another bright spot for the economy is exports. In the first half of 2024, Mexico exported $28 million worth of passenger cars. Car parts, accessories, and trucks were popular exports as well. Avocados and tomatoes were the top food exports to international markets.

CLOSE-UP

## Honoring Independence

The Angel of Independence is a monument in Mexico City. It was built in 1910 to celebrate 100 years since Mexico began its fight for independence. The golden statue on top is called "El Ángel." She holds a victory wreath and a broken chain, which stand for freedom. The monument is about 150 feet (45 m) tall.

In 2024, Claudia Sheinbaum Pardo became the first woman to be elected president of Mexico. She had a lot to do to improve her country. Making the economy stronger, creating a healthcare system that works for everyone, and tackling violence would be among President Pardo's priorities. Affordable energy, reducing pollution, and promoting trade between Mexico and other countries is important, too.

Mexico has seen many changes. It has grown from a rural land to a complex country with both farms and cities. Mexico has a strong past its citizens remember with pride. That pride will move Mexico and its people into the future.

CLOSE-UP

## Day of the Dead

Dia de los Muertos, or the Day of the Dead, is a two-day holiday that begins November 1. On this holiday, families honor members of their family who have passed away. Altars are decorated with marigolds, photographs, and food and drinks.

ALL ABOUT

# MEXICO

**Continent:** North America

**Capital:** Mexico City

**Population:** 132 million

**Official language:** Spanish

**Type of government:** Federal Republic

**Currency:** Mexican peso

**Main religion practiced:** Roman Catholicism

**Colors on Flag:** Green, red, and white

**National bird:** Golden Eagle

# WORDS to Know

| | |
|---|---|
| ancestor | a person from whom one is descended |
| cabinet | a group of people who advise the chief of state |
| cartel | an organization created to control supply or regulate prices of goods or services |
| equitable | fair and impartial |
| hieroglyphic | writing in pictures or symbols instead of words |
| mestizo | a person who has parents of different races |
| nuclear family | a family unit that typically consists of two parents and their children |
| vocational | relating to an occupation or employment |

# LEARN MORE

## Books

Austen, Lily. *Day of the Dead*. Minneapolis, Minn.: Jump!, Inc., 2025.

Dittmer, Lori. *Chichén Itzá*. Mankato, Minn.: Creative Education and Creative Paperbacks, 2025.

O'Neill, Bill. *The Great Book of Mexico: Interesting Stories, Mexican History & Random Facts About Mexico*. Wyoming: Lak Publishing, 2020.

## Websites

"Mexico for Kids." Kids Food Atlas.
https://kidsfoodatlas.com/mexico/

"Mexico." Kids Discover.
https://online.kidsdiscover.com/unit/mexico

"Mexico." National Geographic Kids.
https://kids.nationalgeographic.com/geography/countries/article/mexico

## Documentaries

Aguilar, Pamela, Exec. Prod. *Wonders of Mexico: Mountain Worlds*. Arlington, VA: PBS, 2018.

Cammisa, Rebecca, dir. *Which Way Home*. New York, NY: Documentress Films, 2009.

Rodriguez, Daniela Anelisse, Fabregas, Santiago, and Perez Osorio, Carlos, dirs. *Taco Chronicles*. Mexico City, Mexico: El Estudio, 2019.

Note: Every effort has been made to ensure that any websites listed above were active at the time of publication. However, because of the nature of the Internet, it is impossible to guarantee that these sites will remain active indefinitely or that their contents will not be altered.

# Visit

## CHICHÉN ITZÁ

*Listed as one of the New Seven Wonders of the World, Chichén Itzá is where visitors can see Mayan Ruins in eastern Mexico.*

97751 Yucatán, Mexico

## MUSEUM OF NATURAL HISTORY

*Want to visit a real castle? Chapultepec Castle is home to the Museum of Natural History. It holds over 400 years of Mexican history.*

Bosque de Chapultepec/Secc.
Miguel Hidalgo
11580 Mexico City, Mexico

## MONTE ALBÁN

*Monte Albán is an ancient city built by the Zapotec people. It sits high on a hill in Oaxaca. Visitors can explore old temples, tombs, and plazas that are thousands of years old.*

Ignacio Bernal S/N, 71233 San Pedro Ixtlahuaca, Oax., Mexico

## NATIONAL MUSEUM OF ART

*Visit this museum and see Mexican works of art dating from the 16th to the mid-20th century.*

Tacuba 8
Centro Histórico
Mexico City, 06010

# INDEX